D0368603

The Craptastic Guide to

PSEUDO-SWEARING

Michelle Witte

RUNNING PRESS
PHILADELPHIA · LONDON

© 2012 by Michelle Witte
Published by Running Press,
A Member of the Perseus Books Group

Books published by Running Press are available at special discounts
for bulk purchases in the United States by corporations, institutions, and
other organizations. For more information, please contact the Special Mar-
kets Department at the Perseus Books Group, 2300 Chestnut Street, Suite
200, Philadelphia, PA 19103, or call (800) 810-4145, ext. 5000,
or e-mail special.markets@perseusbooks.com.

ISBN 978-0-7624-4416-8
Library of Congress Control Number: 2011939185

E-book ISBN 978-0-7624-4509-7

9 8 7 6 5 4 3 2 1
Digit on the right indicates the number of this printing

Designed by Jason Kayser
Edited by Cindy De La Hoz
Typography: Encorpada, Futura, and Palatino

Running Press Book Publishers
2300 Chestnut Street
Philadelphia, PA 19103-4371

Visit us on the web!
www.runningpress.com

Cover photo: ©iStockphoto.com/Andrejs Pidjass

Dedication

You know who you are. ::wink::

Table of Contents

Introduction

Dropping a turn-the-air-blue streak of curses can make even the worst situations seem better, but sometimes a *fudge!* or *sugar!* is just as satisfying—and won't land you in trouble.

Masters of fake swearing create pseudo-insults, taunts, and all-purpose swears from seemingly innocent words. Their talent for creative fauxfanity saves them from the dreaded soap-to-mouth wash out.

For those unsure how to fashion believable fake curses without setting their mother's ears on fire, *The Craptastic Guide to Pseudo-Swearing* is here to help. It comes with instructions, helpful hints, exercises, and games to aid in learning. Readers will quickly become prodigious and accomplished fake cursers. It might be the only thing that can save you from shame when putting a nail through your hand while nuns, the elderly, and small children attentively watch nearby.

So remove the bar of soap from your mouth and learn a better way to express how fetchin' mad you get when some son-of-a-biscuit driver flips you the bird—and all without fear of being darned to heck.

WHY FAUXFANITY?

Ah, the illegitimate-son tongue called the English language. It is so very schizophrenic in its heritage. Take a bit of German, throw in some Anglo-Saxon, add a dollop of Latin, then mix with the Romance languages. Don't forget to include a pinch from every language imaginable.

What we get is a living language that rebels against norms and standards. Why, then, are we so worried about *naughty* words? Because they're just that: naughty. You want to be a good boy (or girl), don't you? Don't answer that. The thing is, most people expect to hear polite words when they're out and about in their lives. When you hear a humdinger of a word at places like work, school, or violin practice, it burns the ears. Then the person who said it either has to pretend she doesn't care what others think or apologize profusely while vowing to never ever return, which can be problematic if she wants to keep her job.

That's why this book is here to help. I'm prepared to show you a variety of phrases and words to toss out in a dire moment—and you need never fear reprisal from using one of these terms. Instead, it may bring smiles and even a few chuckles. Who doesn't love to chuckle? So add some variety to your vocab with the creative pseudo-curses presented here. People will surely take notice—in a good way.

TWO FREAKISHLY IMPORTANT NOTES

1.

Fake cursing must be said in all
seriousness, with a straight face, or the impact
of your swears will be lost and
the only reaction you'll get is mockery.

2.

Be confident, especially when
trying out some of the more creative examples.

THE BASICS

There are some hefty words used in this book—and I'm not talking about the loaded terms—so I'll give you a brief guide. I promise, this will come in handy later. (Spoiler: They're language terms. If you know this stuff already, skip ahead to the goods. Also, bravo you! Have a cookie.)

Acronym: A word that originated from the first letter of each word in a phrase.

> *Example*: TGIF! Thank Goodness It's February!

Adjective: Thing that goes in front of a *noun* to modify or change it.

> *Example*: "You *stupid* jerk. Your *fast* car crashed into my *beautiful* wall. You'll pay for this!"

Adverb: Thing that goes in front of a *verb* or *adjective* to change it up (usually ends in "ly").

> *Example*: "He was going so *frickingly* fast, officer. There was no way he could *bleeding* stop in time."

Antonym: The opposite of the first thing.

Example: "Jack was telling me that some *son* of a gun just tried to flirt with our *daughter*."

Dictionary: It has words. Lots of them. And it tells you what they mean. Awesome.

Example: "Merriam-Webster's defines *happy* as—" "Why are you reading the dictionary?" "I have to practice for when I become a politician."

Etymology: The story of what a word means. It's freaking cool, people. Don't be hating on the word nerds.

Example: Once upon a time, there was a little word called Butt. He was a small word, but he often got in trouble for smacking the other kids with his head.

Euphemism: A gentler word used instead of a naughty one.

Example: Pretty much this whole book.

Homonym: Spelled the same but sound different.

> *Example*: "I'm going to *read* this craptastic book on fake swearing. James *read* it and said it's a work of genius."

Homophone: Sound the same when you speak them but are spelled different and have different meanings.

> *Example*: "How could *their* flipping dog crap over *there* when *they're* supposed to be on vacation?"

Interjection: Shout or exclamation. Usually only a single word or short phrase.

> *Example*: "Freak!" "Oh, crap!"

Noun: Person. Place. Thing. Or swamp monster.

> *Example*: "I'll have you know, *sir*, that your *dog* just ate my *cheese 'n' rice* while I was on the *can*. That grates my *cheese*."

Synonym: Means the same as another word.

> *Example*: Synonym is not the same as cinnamon, but it's fun to say them both together really fast. Say it again. One more time. There you go.

Thesaurus: The place where synonyms and antonyms and homonyms all play together in harmony.

> *Example*: "Dude, did you swallow the thesaurus? Maybe you should use small words like *dang* and *darn* before graduating to big stuff like *dagnabbitall to heck*."

Verb: That thing you do.

> *Example*: "Quit *acting* like a fastard." "Don't *talk* to me like that, you meanie!"

TOP TEN

The ten words that follow are the pillars upon which pseudo-swearing is built. Simple words, really, but that's their utter genius. Starting with these words, you can construct elaborate swears that will amaze anyone who is privileged enough to hear them.

Use individually for emphasis and as the staple of your burgeoning vocabulary of swears. Or, slowly build upon one of these swears with the additional words and phrases found throughout the book. But never forget, these words are perfect for nearly every situation because of their quick and effective recall during stress and distress. No need to flounder when the grill explodes, taking the family dinner with it. A simple "Sugar!" expresses the situation with perfect conciseness.

I give you the top ten pseudos . . .

10 **Darn:** "Darnitall!"
(Learn how to build upon this swear on page 48.)

9 **Flip:** "Ah, flip."
(Various forms of this word are found at page 78.)

8 **Dang:** "Dangit!"
(Other examples on page 47.)

7 **Shoot:** "Shoot!"
(For further use, see page 119.)

6 **Gosh:** "Oh my gosh."
(See page 40 for additional info on this swear.)

5 **Fudge:** "Fudge!"
(Learn how to use for maximum impact on page 111.)

4 **Heck:** "Oh my heck!"
(Find more variations of this term on page 45.)

3 **Crap:** "What the crap?"
(See page 94 for more examples.)

2 **Freak:** "What the freak was that?"
(See the versatility of this word on page 80.)

1 **Sugar:** "Oh, sugar!"
(See page 110 for more.)

With this list of fake curses, you're
well on the path to cleaner language. Now go
forth and (pseudo) swear!

FIX-UPS FOR MIX-UPS

Changing habits isn't easy. I feel you. To help you out while you work toward full faux-swearing integration, I've included a helpful sheet on how to switch from real to fake, mid-swear. Just clip it out, photocopy, and tape it wherever you have the greatest desire to swear, like the dashboard of your car, next to the computer keyboard, or beside the baby's crib.

If you catch yourself by the first syllable, you're in good shape to make a successful save.

Go- {
-lly gosh
-sh
}

Da- {
-gnabbit
}

Shhh- {
-ugar
-oot
}

Fuuu- {
-udge
-lip
-reak
-geddaboudit
-or real
-ruit Loops
}

After the first syllable, saves are still possible but must be done with care. Some possible swears that can be adjusted at a later point include:*

- **Beach:** "I just said I want to go to the **beach**."

- **Beehive:** "What do you think about putting a **beehive** in the back yard?"

- **Betcha:** "**Betcha**. Yep, you **betcha**."

- **Dandelion soup:** "Erm, yes. My wife's making **dandelion soup** tonight. Would you like to join us for dinner?"

- **Helvetica:** "**Helvetica**. It's such a great font. I use it at work all the time."

- **Helen of Troy:** "**Helen**'s joining us for dinner. She's from **Troy**, Missouri."

- **Shiitake:** "Ooh boy, **shiitake** mushrooms would make a great addition to that dandelion soup."

- **Fox fake:** "Look at the **fox fake** that woman is wearing!" "At the beach?"

- **Foucault's Pendulum (pronounced foo-co):** "That **Foucault's Pendulum** never knows when to stop."

On rare occasions, an accidental swear can be turned into a cough or sneeze. Just be careful it doesn't sound like an intentional under-the-breath swear. It's a fine line that's easy to cross.

---

* Due to the potentially salacious nature of typing out these transitions from real to fake, we'll leave it to your capable tongue to figure out the appropriate twist.

HOW YOU SAY IT

There's a well-kept secret that pseudo-swearers can use to their advantage: Anything can be a fake curse if you say it right.

Emphasis

Talk about faking it. Learn how to accurately empha-size the wrong syllable and you'll be home free for life. No swear, no soap. *Disclaimer: The Craptastic Guide takes no responsibility for actual results from this advice.*

Example: Holy sheetrock

Mutter under your breath

An excellent tool for all pseudo-swearing needs, the mutter serves several excellent purposes:

1) mumbling adds the air of rebellion and talking back
2) no one knows exactly what was said
3) it's just plain fun.

Example: muttering Bob Saget

Slur the words together

While this is the best way to fake a swear with similar-sounding syllables (say that three times fast, sheesh), it can lead to disaster if slurring results in expressing the actual curse. Proceed with caution.

Example: Cheese 'n' rice

Spit it out

In movies—especially old ones—cowboys all have a piece of hay they're chewing. When they hear the inevitable bad news, they spit their anger—and swear—on the ground. Do the same, but please without the straw and lugey on the floor.

Example: Crap on a stick

Huff

Related to the ever-expressive sigh, the huff lets off steam while adding a sometimes-needed oomph to the simplest of pseudo-curses. In some cases, a plain old huff will more than suffice.

Example: Eff

Look annoyed

Body language is generally louder than words, so why not combine the two for an extra-powerful curse? Try some of these classics: the agitated toe tapping, the hands on hips, the scowl, the single raised eyebrow, and the head shake.

Example: Sweet nibblets (head shake)

Shake a fist

In situations where the intended recipient of the fake curse is too far away to see the more subtle expressions of anger, try the fist shake. It is especially useful when driving (only shake one fist at a time), or while walking away.

Example: Why I oughta . . . (shake fist)

Classic

These swears, well, they've been around awhile. You may have grown up hearing—and using—such common fake swears. Like a classic car, they've only grown better with age. Take a gander at these beauties. Polish 'em up with a little spit shine and they're better than new. They ride smooth through bumpy conversations and make turns around unknown curves with ease. Need something with good mileage? Look no further. These all-purpose swears are perfect for every situation. Why don't you take one for a spin?

Blank

(noun) 1. Nada. Nothing to see here, folks.

2. An empty space. Basically, used when you want to swear, but an adequately vitriolic faux doesn't come to mind. Leave it up to the listener how they'll fill in the *blank. Example:* "What the **blankety blank** are you doing in here? I said to put it in the pantry."

Bleep

(verb) 1. Don't like what someone says? Replace the offending word with an obnoxious sound. Primarily used when someone is speaking, through use of an air horn or alarm buzzer. The same affect can be achieved via text, as shown below. The length of the *bleep* depends on emphasis and how long it takes to shut out offending words. *Example:* Every time that **bleeep** celebrity opens her **bleeeeeep**-ing mouth, those **bleep bleep** censors don't let her actually say **bleeeeeep bleeep** anything. **Bleeeeeeeeeeeeep**!

(noun) 2. An all-purpose sound we've come to know and love. Bleep doesn't just signify a swear, it can actually *be* a swear. *Example:* Oh **bleep**! You **bleeping** fool! What the **bleep** do you mean, officer?

Antonyms: actual words

Etymology: Ah, live TV—an arena ripe for wardrobe malfunctions and slipped swears. Someone with a subversive sense of humor could do all kinds of damage. Around the 1960s, TV stations got wise to the potential for screw-ups and introduced the magnanimous combination of time delay and **bleep**. Basically, it held off broadcasting the show, while an eager prude pressed a bleep button whenever something naughty slipped its way into the broadcast. At least that's how I like to imagine it. Nowadays, some shows use the **bleep** for comedic effect by **bleeping** out words in questionable places, letting viewers fill in the dirty parts themselves. Now how could swearing possibly be funny? Oh, right. That's how.

Curse

(noun) 1. A wish or prayer that something bad will happen, usually to the person being shouted and pointed at. Best said with a loud, declarative voice. For a witch, it's a tactic best used to turn kids into tadpoles and ex-lovers into pond scum. *Example*: I **curse** you, you dastardly devil, to lick the dirt off my toes!" "There's no way I'm licking your toes. That's sick."

2. What villains say when their diabolical plans don't go well. Usually shouted while shaking a fist, generally as the bad guy hightails it outta there. *Example:* "**Curses**! You've won this time, Papa Smurf!"

Cuss

(verb) 1. To say naughty words. *Example:* "Moooomm! Jimmy just **cussed**!" "Which will it be this time, Jim? Dove or Dial?"

2. Yelling. A lot. Usually over something bad or stupid the other person has done. *Example:* Agatha didn't understand why her mother insisted on **cussing** her out. The cat was fine. Nothing a little turpentine couldn't fix.

(noun) 1. Bad word. *Example:* Henry's eyes bulged the first time he heard the big boys use a **cuss**. "Say it again!"

Synonym: swear word; naughty word; dirty word

2. Someone who uses bad words.

3. A bothersome person or animal. *Example:* Don't **cuss** at me, you little **cuss**!

Synonym: potty mouth

Etymology: Cuss probably originated with the word *curse* (surprise, surprise), and the two still share similar meanings. Interestingly enough, it might also have come from a shortening of the word customer. Perhaps the **cuss** isn't always right.

See also: **Curse** (page 30)

Gee

(interjection) 1. Exclamation of surprise.

2. Need to sound innocent? This faux swear is bashful and self-effacing, all in one. This classic has the benefit of diffusing a sticky situation with charm. *Example:* "**Gee**, Mrs. Cleaver. You look swell today." "Put the knife down, Eddie."

Variations: **gee** whiz; golly **gee** willikers; jeepers creepers. *Example*: "**Gee** whiz, G! That's no way to treat a homeboy." "Jeepers creepers! That creepy crawly bug gives me the willies."

See also: **Jeez** (below)

Jeez

(interjection) 1. Gee's second cousin, once removed, Jeez offers a sarcastic element to the otherwise benign exclamation. When spoken, the "e" sound is often drawn out to increase derision.

Example: "**Jeeeeez**, mom. All I did was clean my room, like you asked." "With a leaf blower?"*

2. Also spelled geez or jeeze. Don't worry. The grammar police aren't terribly concerned with misspellings on this one.

Variations: **Jeez** Louise. *Example*: "**Jeez** Louise, Martha. Surely you know I want to marry you!"

Etymology: This puppy has been around since the turn of the twentieth century, so it's a bit on the older side for the classic swears category. But never fear; it serves perfectly in a pinch, especially with the addition of our friendly letter z. Both gee and **jeez** could easily fit in the "Safe for Church" chapter. Add an "us" on the end to understand its origin, though most people don't connect the two anymore.

---

* See page 159 to learn more about the power wielded by our friend the interrobang ‽

TRAILING OFF THE CHARTS

Sometimes a fake swear doesn't need so much of a *bang* ending. In the right situation, a hanging, rolling, or open finish could be the perfect way to fake a swear. Take, for instance, a zombie apocalypse.

"How the . . . " said while staring at the decomposing bodies regaining animation is much more realistic than a long string of elaborate swears. You are, of course, too busy trying to keep chomping teeth away from your Chihuahua to care about eloquence. So when the zombie hordes have been neutralized and you're ready to settle in for a nice cup of chocolate, only to see a swarm of alien invaders descending on your front lawn, **"Who the . . . "** is the perfect response. By the time your nephew sprouts wings from his new genetic mutations, you're ready to trail off with, **"Son of a . . . "** (*See also* "What the . . . on page 36.) No missteps here. You've got this formula down pat.

Since Craptastic headquarters is always prepared to welcome new paranormal overlords, we've prepared a chart of possible causes worldwide destruction and/or devastation, and the appropriate trailing swears (see page 36). Just remember: the key to a good trailing swear is the implied question or exclamation. Body language is also a great addition. Severe shock is an excellent option for facial expression. In the case of a disaster of biblical proportions, rending of clothing or tearing of hair is especially appropriate.

IT'S APOCA–FREAKIN'–LYPTIC!

TRAILING SWEAR

WHAT THE...   ....

WHO THE...   ....

HOW THE HECK...   ....

SON OF A...   ....

WHERE IN THE WORLD...   ....

WHY...   ....

NOOOOO...   ....

CATASTROPHIC EVENT

Opening of Hellmouth	Extermination byDaleks	Overthrown by Fairies
Alien invasion	Viking abduction	Enslavement by Cylons
Controlled by parasitic creatures	Zombie apocalypse	Water turns to blood
Rash of genetic mutations	overthrown by robots	Locust swarm
Dolphins develop legs & overtake the land	Overrun by bunny horde	Land ravaged by dragons
Melting of polar caps	Nature reclaiming Earth	Plague
Nuclear holocaust	Solar implosion	Vampire feast

Safe for Church

Religious-based swears have long dominated the world's vocabulary. Why, even the word profanity comes from the Latin term meaning "outside the temple"; basically, things that don't belong in a church. Huh, go figure. Anyway, such religious language has long resulted in "minced oaths," or as we like to call them, pseudo-swears!

Yesiree. There are plenty of folks who don't like to hear words of a sacred variety used for not-so-special purposes, so over the years those words have been tweaked until only excellent faux curses remain.

English speakers aren't the only ones who use religious language to tint the air blue. Hey, speaking of blue, what about that French phrase *sacre bleu* (sacred blue). Doesn't make much sense—unless you know that *Dieu* is the French word for God. It's one of those tricksy pseudos, where it sounds alike so you're not really swearing when you swear.

Gosh

(interjection) 1. No need to explain this one, really. Even those who don't regularly mince their swears know what this one means—and maybe even use it.

2. Mainly used to express surprise, delight, or even anger. *Examples*: **Gosh** darnitall to heck in a handbag! Good **gosh**! "Oh my **gosh**, Becky. Look at her butt. It is sooo big."

Golly

(interjection) 1. This one's a touch old fashioned, but if you need to feign a bit of innocence, let 'er rip.

2. Works as a great accompaniment to the word gosh. *Examples*: **Golly Gosh!** By **golly**! "**Golly** gee wilikers, sir. I didn't mean to turn the hose on your grandmother." "Good **golly**, Miss Molly! Oh, sorry. I mean Mr. Smith."

Variations: **golldarnit**, **gulldernit**

Egad

(interjection) 1. This is a bit more high fallutin' than most, but it's a great alternative for when gosh just isn't enough.

Variations: **egads**, **gadzooks**

Dog

(noun) 1. A cute little ball of fur that grows up to be a very large shedding pile of fur.

Example: "**Doggonit**, who let Fido sleep on the bed? Now I have to comb my pillow before I can sleep."

(interjection) 1. Fortunately, this mutt word won't slobber all over you, though it can be a cute word for exclamation purposes.

2. Warning: Those who wrestle with dyslexia may want to avoid this one. Getting it backward may result in a hand slapping—or the soap. *Example:* "By **dog**, I'm tired, Rover. Why don't *you* push *me* in the wheelbarrow for a bit?"

Devil

(noun) 1. Big bad meanie who lives in a very heckish place. *Example:* "Ah, **devil** take you!" "Why thank you for the invitation. I think I shall. Come along, Timmy."

(interjection) 1. Not quite as all-purpose as heck, it's still a good word for those times when you want to call out someone on devilish behavior. *Example:* "What the **devil** are you doing to the dog? He's not supposed to fly!"

Doggonit

GREAT EXCLAMATIONS!

How is it that an author dedicated to improving society got stuck with being another name for the Biggest Bad Guy of All Time? What the **dickens** does it even have to do with Charles Dickens? Well, nothing, really. It wasn't about him. That expression had been around long before the celebrated Mr. Dickens was born, maybe even hundreds of years. Basically, no one knows why, but it's sure fun to make up a story to explain it. Go on. Take a crack at it. Make Dickens proud.

WHAT THE DICKENS?

Heck

(noun) 1. A very hot and fiery place where you probably wouldn't want to spend much time. The neighbors tend to be a bit cranky since they're burning in eternal torment. Plus the little pitchfork-toting folk tend to be a lively bunch. *Example*: "Go to **heck**, you little hellions!"

2. Supposedly, one place that is capable of emotion. *Example:* "I'm mad as **heck**, and I won't stand for it!" "Then sit down."

(interjection) 1. As a swear, this all-purpose word can't be beat. Use it whenever—and wherever—you'd like. *Examples*: "What the **heck** happened here? I just looked out the window a second ago. There's no way you kids are that big of troublemakers." "Ah, **heck**! There she goes again. Grandma! Your pants!"

Why swear when you can spell? Obviously, the hockey sticks make it a faux swear. Say it with L's and you're on your own with the soap, bud. *Example*: "**H-E-double hockey sticks**! He just got hit in the face with a puck!"

Hades

(noun) 1. Like its cousin heck, Hades is *the* destination for the Greeks in afterlife. In this place, though, both good and bad congregate together. Equality for eternity, I suppose. *Example*: "**Hades**, I can't believe we got out of there alive. No more all-you-can-eat buffet. Ever."

2. Not just a place, but the person who the place is named after. Wait, what? *Example*: "What the **hades** am I going to do with you, Pluto? I told you to stay off the table! Oh, dog."

Dang

(verb) 1. In the strictest sense, it means you've been naughty and are being sent to heck.

2. In another sense, you've been naughty and are being sent to your room without dinner.

3. Experts are not sure which is worse. *Examples*: "**Dang** it! He sunk my battleship!" "Well, I'll be **danged**. He's a superhero. I just thought he had a fetish for multicolored tights. **Dang** you, Superman! Your perfectly sculpted and attired abs have ruined me again!"

Variation: **dagnabbit**. *Example*: No sentence for this one because, well, it's just so much fun to say by itself. **Dagnabbit**!

Darn

While nearly always used interchangeably with *dang*, differences in pronunciation make it worthy of its own entry. For instance, some swear phrases just sound better with *darn*. So, basically, copy everything I said about dang and repeat it here. (What? I'm too lazy to do it myself.) *Example*: "**Darnitall** to heck. He just stole my knitting needles!"

Etymology: Often, **darn** is used as a tamer version of—er—another word, which we won't repeat. But what if it also descended from a word meaning "secret"? Ooh, now doesn't that sound scintillating? The secret to "tarnation." Or maybe that's not what they meant. Either way, it's safe to bet that you won't get too much flack for using this word, especially if you're discussing socks in the same sentence.

Tarnation

(verb) 1. What happens when you're darned.
Example: "Well how in **tarnation** was I supposed to
know that? It's not like I pay my taxes."

Variation: **Dalmatian**. *Example*: "What the **Dalmatian**
do you think you're doing? You know you're not
allowed to use the fireman carry on your father."

Need a reason to switch to pseudo swears? How about a few days in the stocks. Yikes. That's the reason some scholars think milder forms of common swears started popping up after colonists landed in America. (Those silly pilgrims, penalizing people for foul language.) It's not like we fine TV stations millions of dollars for broadcasting naughty words. Oh, wait . . . Hey, someone should send a copy of this book to those TV execs. We'd save them so much money. Yes, dear readers, *Craptastic* is doing its best to save the world.

LOVE, GOODNESS, AND ALL THAT'S HOLY

For the love

(euphemism) 1. Great way to show exasperation. Generally involves someone doing something really stupid. *Example*: "Oh, **for the love**! I did not say you could tie your brother to the roof."

2. Sometimes the names that appear at the end of this phrase are of early Christian saints. *Example*: "**For the love** of Mike! I wanted one pickle, not two!"

3. A further variation changes it from "for the love of" to "for the sake of" or, shorter, "for _____'s sake." *Example*: "I just need a glue gun that doesn't burst into flame, **for craft's sake**."

4. Why not shorten it even more? Just use "for _____." Easy peasy. *Example*: "Stop your crying, **for crying out loud**!"

Wanna see something cool? Watch how this common phrase has changed over time: For the love of all that's good and holy → For Pete's sake → For pity's sake → For the love of Pete → For the love of Peter, Paul, and Mary → For the love . . .

Goodness

(noun) 1. Another of the "golly" and "gosh" euphemisms. Use at will. *Example*: "Be good, for **goodness' sake**, or an old fat man will creep into your bedroom at night and stare at you while you sleep."

Some excellent phrases that utilize **goodness**:

- **Goodness** gracious!
- Oh my **goodness**!
- Thank **goodness**.

Synonyms: **gosh**; **golly**

HOLY GUACAMOLE

While some may say an entry on holy words in a book filled with faux swears is wholly irreverent, I like to think we made a hole in one with this addition. Why, there are so make fakes around here, it's a wonder there isn't a whole book out of this one section alone. Nah. While there are plenty of holies (and holes) around, there probably aren't enough to justify a whole book. But more to the point, what's up with all this holy shiz? Hmm. Looks like we'll have to put this whole phenomenon to a *Craptastic* test.

- **Holy moly:** It appears that the creators of the *Captain Marvel* comic made up this phrase. I support anyone who can come up with a new word that people actually use.

- **Holy guacamole:** Well, avocados have pits, which, when removed, leave a large hole. So, sure, guacamole can be holy.

- **Holy cow:** Hey! This one actually makes sense. There are some cultures that consider cows holy, most famously Hindus in India. Okay, fine. You can keep this one.

- **Holy Toledo:** Is Toledo, Ohio, holier than any other city in the world? Apparently so.

- **Holy Hannah:** Some names are better than others, it seems. So to all you Hannahs out there, congrats on being superior to the rest of us. It's not like we care. Jerks.

- **Holy smoke:** Since smoke particles get mixed in the air and there are plenty of breathing holes once it starts to dissipate, this passes the *Crap* test.

- **Holy crap:** Dang it! If this whole test is crap, then this one *has* to pass.

And then it devolves into gibberish. At least the first two rhyme . . .

- **Holy majoly**
- **Holy tamoli**
- **Holy schnikeys**

Well, that went rather . . . er, nevermind. Moving on. Since our holy examination didn't quite pan out, why don't we just throw the whole concept to the wind and make up our own swears. Cause we totally haven't been doing that . . . yet. Almost anything can become saintly if "holy" is stuck to the front. By themselves, these things are rather boring and ordinary. But add a drop of holy and you get objects that are much more fascinating:

- **Holy folks**
- **Holy socks**
- **Holy rhinoceros**
- **Holy bat on a stick**
- **Holy crap on a cracker**

WHAT THE WHAT?

A fairly all-purpose prefix, "what the" can turn even the most innocuous words into legitimate faux-swears. The most common involve the classic curses—heck, crap, freak—but recent usage is dominated by creativity. Nearly any object can become the subject of a "**What the . . .** " phrase.

What the toy soldier?

What the Mazda?

What the rainbow-barfing unicorn?

To take it a step further, use clever combinations of swears to add a boost to a tired curse.

What the crap?

becomes

What the crap-flinging monkey?

However, we must never forget the impact an incomplete phrase can have in the right situation. (See page 36 for a handy chart of other unfinished swears.) Upon first seeing a sea monster rampaging on land, "**What the . . .** " trailing off and followed by screams is most effective. To create your own "**What the . . .** " swear, make sure the object of the sentence *is* an object; otherwise, it won't make much sense. Take it for a spin and see how it feels in your mouth. You won't be disappointed.

What the _____ ?

What the _____ _____ ?

Note: This phrase is even more potent in writing when accompanied by an interrobang (see page 158).

PLAY IT SAFE

Don't forget the hat and cravat, plus each eye, ear, finger, and toe!

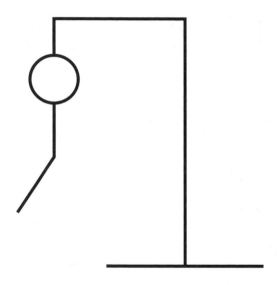

S H _ _   _ H _
F _ O _ _   _ O O _
  _ O _   _ O _
O F   _   _ _ _ _ H

HECK: where the bad letters go

P M I Z Q

See page 167 for answer.

Mothers & Sons

Why do moms get such a bad rap? It's not like your mom is so bad, right? Right? Then why all the mommy issues? Mom curses range from the totally offensive to the downright insulting "Yo mama so fat . . ." I think it's time to cut moms a little slack.

Remember how she baked you cookies and kissed your scraped knees? Is this any way to thank your dear sweet mother for all the long hours she spent in labor, sweating and (pseudo) cursing in agony just so you could take your first breath? And why don't you call her? Have you grown so big in your britches that you can't even pick up a phone to let her know you're not lying dead in a ditch somewhere? Now go give your mother a big kiss while we discuss these swears.

Mother

(noun) 1. Female humanoid that has taken care of you since you were a parasitic fetus swimming around in her stomach.

2. All encompassing swear that should not be used in the presence of your mother. *Example*: "**Mother**! I didn't say you could come out of your cage."

3. Attempt to establish the lineage of a particular person.

Example: "**Mother of pearl**, that hurt!" "No, dear. My daughter's name is Ruby."

Variation: sweet **mother of vinegar**

Your mom

(noun) 1. A popular retort. Flows in a similar vein to "Yo mama so fat."

2. Best said with a slight inflection on "your"; i.e., "yer mom." *Example*: "Who put the phone in the fridge?" "**Your mom**." "You're probably right. She is a bit forgetful."

MOMMY LOVES YOU

Would you kiss your mother with a filthy mouth? We think not. Which is why we've compiled a list of suitable substitutes for a rather popular phrase. The following faux swears are fairly self-explanatory, though some become more apparent once said out loud. 'Nuff said.

- **Mother father**
- **Mother trucking**
- **Mother hugger**
- **Mother licker**
- **Mother lover**
- **Motor scooter**
- **Monkey fighting**
- **Monday to Friday**

Witch

(noun) 1. Older woman with scoliosis who is prone to growing warts on her nose. Also obsessed with cleaning, as evidenced by the broom she carries with her wherever she goes. *Example*: "That **witch** turned me into a newt!" "Sure. Whatever you say. Why don't we go have a nice visit with my doctor friend?"

2. Term popularized by prepubescent girls. Often, their first attempt at swearing, fake or real. *Example*: "You're such a . . . a **witch with a B**!" "I'll have you know, I get straight As."

3. A swear that has taken over an entire letter in the alphabet: B. *Example*: "You stupid **B**. Quit buzzing in my ear." "I did no such thing! Hmph!"

Variations: **beehive**, **beach**

See also: **curse** (page 30).

Son

(noun) 1. The offspring of a mother.

2. Yet again with the mommy issues. While generally said to a male person, the implication is that it's the mother's fault. Why don't we just agree that moms are great and they have nice sons. See? All happy. *Example*: "Get back here, you **son of a witch**!" "Hey! My mother may cast spells on occasion, but that doesn't mean she's a witch. Okay, it does."

Alternate spelling: **sunnuva**

Variation: **son of a gun**, **son of a bench**

(interjection) 1. This really has nothing to do with sons or mothers. It's just fun to shout. *Example*: "**Son of a** . . . Exactly how did the dog get up that tree?"

Somehow over the years witches turned into ditches. It's probably that whole rhyming thing. Anyway, it's given us oath mincers some choice phrases to shout at will. You can probably shout them at John too. Maybe even Henrietta. **Slug in a ditch**; **Swan in a ditch**

Fastard

(noun) 1. Younger brother of son of a . , , , 2. Again with the mommy issues. Sheesh. Do we need to get out the coat hanger again? *Example*: "Don't call me a **fastard**!" "Fine then. How about slowtard?"

Variation: **buzzard**

SON OF A . . .

With all this talk of mothers and their sons, it makes you wonder what these men, er, boys, er, males should really be called. A goose mom that has baby girl geese would call them goslings, so naturally the son of a goose would be a bosling. See? Totally different. But what would the rest of these sons be called?

Son of a beach ball

_____

Son of a biscuit-eating bulldog

_____

Son of a building block

_____

Son of a bun

_____

Son of a cheesemaker

_____

Son of a peach

_____

See page 167 for answers.

SHOW OFF YOUR PROWESS WITH . . . RASSAFRACKIN' ROAD RAGE!

With this handy guide, you'll have a bevy of appropriate phrases for every stressful driving situation. But remember: always keep a cool head and steady hands while driving. I'm talking to you, middle finger.

You get cut off:

> "You're going down, you **son of a biscuit-eating bulldog**!"

You get in a fender bender:

> "**Stupid B**!"

As you race through a yellow-not-quite-red light:

> "**Son of a** . . . Hold on tight!"

> *Also appropriate*: "Eeeeeee!"

You get pulled over for speeding*:

> "**Swan in a ditch**!"

A car is tail-gaiting you:

"Freaking fastard!"

You get a ticket for not using your blinker**:

"Dad gum mother licker!"

Some idiot zooms by to cut to the front of the line of standstill cars even though you courteously moved into the other lane after seeing that three lanes were closed up ahead***:

"Mother of pearl!"

You pull the hood release instead of the emergency brake while driving down the freeway, making it hard to see once the hood smashes against the windshield****:

"Sweet mother vinegar!"

---

* Wisely said before rolling down the window to speak to the nice police officer.

** Also known as a linker, blinking light thingie, or turn signal.

*** I'm not bitter.

**** It really happened. Twice. To the same person. No, it wasn't me.

Sexy Talk

Talk about family relationships: the mother of all swears just entered the room. I bet you don't even need me to tell you the first letter of her name to know what I'm talking about. Yep, this swear is so well known—and avoided—that it rules over a letter of the alphabet. Sheesh. That word packs one frigging large punch.

You might be surprised to learn that this taboo word has been around since the fifteenth century, which means people have been finding ways to *not* say it for just as long. Heck, even Shakespeare danced around this humdinger of a bad word (see page 146). Here at *Craptastic*, we've done the dirty work to bring you suitable substitutes to this bomb-diggity swear. Read on, dear swearer, and fear not. No such foul language shall appear within these pages, but that doesn't mean we can ignore the prominent—and readily transparent—replacements many use today.

BROUGHT TO YOU BY THE LETTER "F"

F

(interjection) 1. Mother of all swears. Bombs away!

2. 'Nuff said. *Example*: "**FU**!" "I've never heard of that university. Is that in Florida?"

(verb) 1. Add an -ing on the end, and it's an all-inclusive verb good for any situation. *Example*: "Oh my **f-ing g**! Did you really dye your hair polka dot?"

Alternate spelling: **eff**

Variation: **F off**

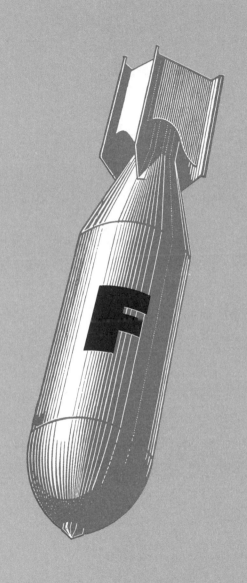

Still a little too close to the **F bomb** for comfort? Never fear! We've scoured the **f-ing** globe to bring you the finest **f-ing** replacements.

Forget

(verb) 1. To forget about remembering someone or something.*

2. Dismiss someone completely. *Example*: "Aw, **forget this**. I don't need English class no more. I know my ABDs."

"**Forget you**." "Sweetie, you've got it wrong. *I'm* the one who forgot to pick *you* up from school."

---

*Are we allowed to define a word with that same word? Hold onto your seats. We might be entering paradox territory.

HIT THE ROAD, G

Most of the words in this section can be used extensively as modifiers for other swears by adding an -ing to the end. Often, the phrase is said with a silent "g" as in "frickin' heck!" Exclamation points are required.

- **Oh my freaking heck!**
- **Fetching bullspit!**
- **That's flipping awesome!**
- **I'm so fricking there!**
- **No frigging way!**

Fetch

(interjection) 1. Throwing a stick is not a require-
ment for using this term, though if it makes you
feel better, go for it. *Example*: "What the **fetch** did you
do that for? I just bought ten gallons of cologne."

Variation: **fletch** (part of arrow)

Flip

(interjection) 1. Frequently used to show embarrass-
ment or frustration. *Example*: "Ah, **flip**, mom. Why'd
you meet my date in your bathrobe and curlers?"
"Because I **abso-flippin'-lutely** love to see my itty-
bitty boy blush."

Flying

(adjective) 1. This use of the word has nothing to do with flying, though that's much cooler than it being a descriptive term added onto a noun for emphasis. *Example*: "I don't give a **flying** monkey's butt if you're tired. We're not leaving until I see the baby penguins."

Variation: **fox fake**, **ferrets**

Freak

(interjection) 1. Generally shouted in anger or frustration. *Example*: "**Freak**, that's loud! Can't you turn the volume down on that thing?" "Babies don't come with remotes."

(noun) 1. A descriptor of a place or thing that isn't considered normal. Not to be used regarding people, cause that's just not nice. *Example*: "What the **flying car**? **Freak of nature**!" "It's actually pretty natural for a tornado to pick up a car and fling it at high speeds." "Not *our* car!"

Variation: **fork, fire truck**

Frick

(interjection) 1. This word can be said quickly and with minimal effort, so it's an excellent choice for situations where you must swear in haste. *Example*: "What the **frick** was that?" "Calm down. It's only my sand dollar. He was hungry."

(adjective) 1. Best used to highlight something exciting or interesting. *Example*: "That's **fricking** weird. I swear I put the lid back on the jar of newt eyes."

Variation: **frickity frack**

See also: **frak** (page 145)

Frig

(interjection) 1. Show contempt for something despicable. *Example*: "**Friggin-A**, that hurt! No more trapezing for me."

2. Excellent way to show complete disregard for something. Should not be confused with a boat (frigate). *Example*: "Ah, **frig it**! There's no way I'm trudging through snow uphill both ways just to go to school."

3. To mess around or with something. What a mess. *Example*: "Don't **frig** around with me, you stupid boat."

Variation: **frag**

See also: **fragging aardvarks** (page 142)

Fug

(interjection) 1. Proper pronunciation of this faux-fanity is essential, or you could otherwise end up with a red handprint on your cheek.

2. It might be best to use this term as part of another phrase, to avoid that likelihood. *Example*: "That was **freaking fugtastic**! Who knew parakeets were such good drivers?"

Etymology: This euphemism owes its popularity to the writer Norman Mailer. Back in 1948, the publishers of his book *The Naked and the Dead* weren't too keen on using real swears—of which there were quite a few—so they made him change the language up a bit, using the word **fug** instead. But, honestly, the word is a bit **fugly** to the ears. Couldn't he have chosen **flip** or **fetch** instead?

Variations: **flug, flub**

Suck

(verb) 1. A personal favorite here at *Craptastic*, **suck** is a great, all-encompassing verb. Show off with this swear.

2. Also an excellent choice when showing disdain or fed-up-ness. *Example*: "This **sucks**! Why did the hurricane have to land right in the middle of my birthday party? We didn't even get cake yet!"

(interjection) 1. Possesses a flair that accents any dire situation. *Example*: "Ah **suck**! I just wanted to dominate the world. Is that too much to ask?"

Variation: **blows, bites**

F UNIVERSITY

In the *Craptastic* endeavor to promote learning and knowledge, we present a few tidbits about the Word that Must Not Be Said. Don't worry. No need to shield your eyes. We keep things clean here at *Craptastic*.

There isn't a word in the English language more polarizing than this one. As we already mentioned, it is so volatile that everyone knows it by a single letter of the alphabet. Hint: the F word.

This is one adaptable word, used in nearly every part of speech: noun (person, place, *and* thing), verb (both transitive and intransitive*), adjective, and adverb. Some people even say it so much, it seems like it's the only word they know. Or the only one they use with regularity.

There are many apocryphal stories about how this Worst of All Words came to be. Some say it was an acronym from the Dark Ages, when the populace was trying to rebuild after the Black Death. So they had to get "**C**onsent from the **K**ing to **F**ornicate." The word **U**nder might be part of that phrase as well. The other tale has several variations, but all share the same theme of adulterers or criminals of a naughty nature being marked "**F**or having **K**nowledge of **U**nlawful, and usually **C**arnal things."

Modern scholars don't really agree with these stories as being the genesis of the F bomb. Instead, some cite Germanic origins. The English language itself is actually Germanic based, so this makes a lot of sense. Let's just say, though, that this particular word came from other words meaning similar things.

It has been around a looooong time, some say the fifteenth century; others believe it dates back even earlier, to the 1200s. It's pretty much always had the taboo it holds today, though much less now than in previous eras. For centuries, it wasn't even written down. Dictionaries finally started printing it without dashes or asterisks in the late 1960s and early '70s.

Many of the current phrases that utilize this ever-present word have one major contributor: the military. Yep. You heard it right. Those boys really do swear like sailors. (Har har.) One of the most prevalent phrases that has since gone into general use is **snafu** (a **N**ormal **S**ituation got **A**ll messed **U**p or **F**udged). The origin of the word seems to have been forgotten by most of the population; otherwise it might not be so commonly used.

In the modern era, this word is making more of an appearance, both written and heard. But as that word becomes more visible, fake swears are rising in popularity right along with it.

Vive le faux-swear!

---

*No, you can't buy a ticket for the intransitive or transitive railroads. Do not pass go, do not collect $200.

MIX 'N' MATCHIN' &*%&^

Take one swear from each column to create a super-powerful—and personalized—curse.

What the . . .	**Freaking**
Son of a . . .	**Stupid**
For the . . .	**Holy**
By . . .	**Dag**
What in . . .	**Jeepers**
Oh my . . .	**Frackin'**
How in the . . .	**Bloody**
Sweet . . .	**Sufferin'**
Why I'll . . .	**Fetchin'**

Goat	in a boat
Nature	on a cracker
Face	-lutely
Fudge	out loud
Bullspit	on a stick
Scrud	-tastic
Cheese	in a can
Beachball	to heck
Monkey	is holy
	face

Potty Mouth

Over the years, language sure has gone down the toilet. What's behind it all? Well, the potty is one of those places you just can't avoid, no matter how hard you try. (Please don't try!) Seeing as it's a universal, er, problem, it makes sense that people would use those words for things other than for which they were originally intended.

So kick it in the posterior with these not-quite-so-foul words. And don't worry. We'll go light on the definitions. No need to send you to the bathroom more than is necessary.

UNMENTIONABLES

Butt

(noun) 1. Tush.

2. Swears generally add this word onto any object, though body parts seem to be most popular.

Variations: **butt head**, **butt hole**, **butt munch**

Synonym: **A**

A

(noun) 1. Another term for the posterior, though this one is shortened from a not-so-long real swear.

2. These swears run a wider gamut, with fauxfanities describing both a person or thing *as* the rear element, or how the swearer will beat upon said end. To wit:

- **Dumb A**
- **Kick your asphalt; Astroturf; astronaut**
- **A-hole**

Example: "Why don't you come a little closer, space man, so I can kick your **astronaut**!"

Continuing with the theme of orifices, here are some other choice terms that can be used:

- **Grass hole**
- **Ice hole**
- **Sasquatch hole**

Example: "Don't be such a **grass hole**, you stupid ball! Just drop into the cup so I can move on to the ninth hole."

Crap

(noun) 1. Slightly stinky as a swear, this rather potent object can knock a man off his feet if he isn't careful.

2. There are so many variations on this word alone, and we haven't even started on its close cousins, **crud** and **bull**.

- **Crappy**
- **Crappola**
- **Craptastic**
- **Craptacular**
- **Crapdoodle**
- **Crap on a stick**

Example: "Look, mom! It's the most **craptastically craptacular pile of crap** book on the planet." "Put it down, son, and walk away. Quickly."

Crud

(noun) 1. Oh, fine. The cousins can have their own entries too. No one in the family wants a **crapstorm** of jealousy. It takes so long to clean up the mess. *Example*: "What's that sign say?" "Let's see: 'Beware the **crud monkey**, which takes pride in flinging itself around.' "

CRUD MONKEYS!

Bull

(noun) 1. A rather large and angry animal that produces large steaming piles of, well, bull crap.

2. The visuals in this chapter just keep getting better and better.

3. Often refers to lies or untruths.

Variations: big steaming **load of bull**, **bull crap**, **bull dip**, fetching **bullspit**, **BS**

Example: "John, I'm calling **BS**! **BS**! You liar!" "Whoa, kid. It's just a card game. If you'd prefer, we can go back to Old Maid." "But I like shouting **BS**!"

HOW MANY WAYS CAN YOU SAY IT?

CHIZZ

DOO

BULL

CRAP

SHIZ

SHIDT

POO

POOP

PUCKY

POO POO

SHIH TSU

CRUD

SCRUD

UNNATURAL DISASTERS

There are moments in life when the poo hits the fan and sprays all over your nice white furniture. It's times like these when a simple curse just isn't enough. This is crap of epic proportions. What follows are emphatic descriptors to show just how bad things are.

Brown out

Poocano

Crap storm

Shizzicane

Hurricrap

H

Shizzard

Poonado

Poonami

L

Poovalanche

Chizzclone

ON THE OTHER END OF THE SPECTRUM IS THE DIXIE CUP . . .

Pee

(noun) 1. As we've crossed the Mason-Dixon line toward Dixie land, it should be noted that there are much fewer terms on this side.

2. Generally, these terms refer to anger or other volatile emotions.

- Piddle
- Peeved
- PO'd
- Ticked off
- TO'd

Example: "You've crossed me for the last time, Mason!" "Well, you've **peeved me off**, Dixon!"

DOWN THE CRAPPER

We owe a lot to Sir Thomas Crapper, the least of which is the pseudo-swear named after this Victorian plumber. Sometimes credited as the inventor of the modern toilet, Crapper dedicated his life to the art of poop disposal.

I can't think of a better homage to such a devoted plumber than to be named for the principle object of his occupation: poo.

It's craptastic!

To honor this hardy soul, use the word proudly and often, and as loud as is decent. Hooray for plumbing! Two cheers for streets void of raw sewage! Let's give him a shout:

DEM SWEARS

To explain the complicated workings of the digestive
tract and its impact on pseudo-swearing, I've included a
helpful song, to the tune of the old African-American
spiritual "Dem Bones." This requires reader participa-
tion, so prop the book up on a table, stretch your
muscles, and prepare to sing along. Bonus points for
creative actions.

Chorus
Dem swears, dem swears, dem pseudo-swears.
Dem swears, dem swears, dem pseudo-swears.
Dem swears, dem swears, dem pseudo-swears.
Make me a potty mouth.

Let's make dem swears, dem pseudo-swears.
Let's make dem swears, dem pseudo-swears.
Let's make dem swears, dem pseudo-swears.
Come out my potty mouth.

Nose holes connected to de mouth hole.
Mouth hole connected to de throat chute.
Throat chute connected to de tummy.
Tummy connected to de innards.
Innards connected to de poop hole.
Dey also connected to de pee hole.
So now we pseudo-swear.

Chorus

De piddle and de wee come out de Dixie cup.
De crud and de crap come out de A-hole.
Innards make it into a pile o' shiz.
Tummy churn up all de Cheez Whiz.
Mouth hole make things all barftastic.
Nose holes smell all de bull spit.
Behold my potty mouth.

PO'D PICTURES

Spice up your game night with this craptacular version of Pictionary. Simply replace the blasé words from the traditional game with frickin' awesome pseudo-swears. Some suggestions are below, but get adventurous and make up your own. Just remember: the longer—and stranger—the phrase, the funnier the drawing. Ready, set, go!

- Mother Hubbard
- Crud monkeys
- Fridge magnet
- Son of a cheesemaker
- Flippin' heck
- Jumpin' Jehosephat
- Doody head
- Fiddlesticks
- Lint licker

PRACTICE SHEET

Eat Your Words

Oh, sweet sugar. How drab life would be without you. And yet, we still take our desserts for granted. That's not the only food group, either. Somehow we've turned our munchies into fauxfanities. Don't believe me? Take a look at the helpful chart that follows:

BASIC FOOD GROUPS

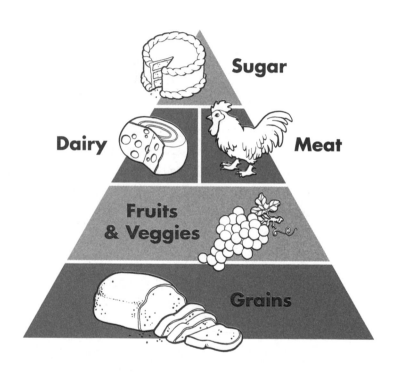

Sugar

Dairy

Meat

Fruits & Veggies

Grains

Sugar

Bull sugar
Sugar head
Sweet nibblets
Fruit Loops
Fudge
Mother fruitcake

Meat

Baloney
Cheeseburger
Good gravy
Oh carp
Fish sticks
Holy mackerel

Fruit & Veggies

Applesauce
Dundelion soup
Shiitake
Sweet mother gherkin

Grains

Son of a biscuit-eating bulldog
What the French toast?
Holy macaroni
Holy crap on a cracker

Dairy

Mother's milk
Soft cheeses
Cheese 'n' rice
Cheese in a can

Cheesed off
Cheez Whiz
Holy cheese and crackers
Kraft Dinner

Sugar

(noun) 1. These sucrose crystals are too sweet to pass up.

2. The most important food group, vital for emotional health.

(interjection) 1. Excellent swear for most occasions and sweet enough that shouts of surprise won't earn dirty glares. *Example*: "**Sugar**! I just spilled salt all over the table."

Synonym: **sweet**

Antonym: **crap**

See also: **fudge** (page opposite)

Fudge

(noun) 1. Ooey gooey chocolatey goodness.

2. Ambrosia of the gods.

(interjection) 1. Short and sweet with just one syllable, it's the perfect way to express frustration. *Example*: "Ah, **fudge**. Who ate all the brownies?"

Variations: **mercy fudge**, **fudgesicle**, **fudgetastic**

YOU ARE WHAT YOU EAT

There was this one time when my mom decided to eat only carrots because of this fad diet going around. She ate so many carrots . . . her skin started turning *orange*! I swear it's true. No, there's no photographic evidence. No, I didn't see it. But seriously, my dad told me, so it *must* be true.

It's a good thing she stopped, or at this very moment, I might be sporting the best permanent fake tan this side of L.A. Talk about baby carrots.

Anyway, where were we? Carrots . . . food . . . Oh, yes! Food. We were discussing how the things you put into your mouth can turn you into large vegetables. But think about the inverse. What if—now this might be a bit of a stretch—the things that come *out* of your mouth determine what kind of person you are.

No, I'm not talking about spit or vomit. Gross. But what about those little word things that pop out of your mouth whenever you talk? You know what I'm saying. Of course I'm saying words. Yeesh. Just think about what those words mean.

Would you *eat* garbage? Carp no! Then why would you say it? Ha ha! Got you there! To overstate the point, here's a handy diagram that oversimplifies the discussion:

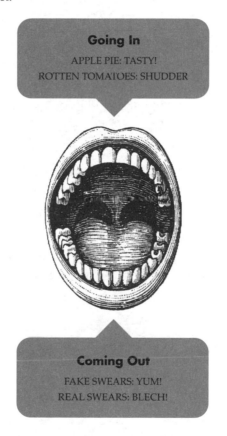

Going In
APPLE PIE: TASTY!
ROTTEN TOMATOES: SHUDDER

Coming Out
FAKE SWEARS: YUM!
REAL SWEARS: BLECH!

PSEUDO-SANDWICH

Fake swearing is hard work, you know. So we're taking a lunch break. Join us if you'd like. On the menu today are Pseudo Sandwiches. Here's how it goes: We're taking fairly regular words and making them fake-tacular with our special Pseudo-Sandwich maker. Well, they're not actually slices of bread. This book would go stale much too quickly if we did that. Instead, we're using words.

Take the first slice of bread (part of the word), fill with your preferred faux-swear, then sandwich with the second slice. Voila! Pseudo-Sandwich! For the best flavor, use any of the swears in this book that end with -ing for the filling.

It's *un*-fricking-*believable*! Don't believe me? Try one yourself. Here's a good one for you. Ready?

Fan- _____ **-tastic!**

Oh, yum. These sandwiches are excellent. Why don't you help yourself to a few more as we go get things ready for the next chapter. We left the fixings out. Just throw them back in the fridge when you're done.

Abso- _____ **-lutely**

Fan- _____ **-tastic**

Guaran- _____ **-tee**

Posi- _____ **-tively**

Un- _____ **-believable**

CROSS WORDS PUZZLE

ACROSS

2. A saintly fish.
3. This bird couldn't find a better place to swim.
5. These primates like to throw poo.
6. It's not a pug, but you can say this when the dog pees on the carpet.
7. Agreeing with a font.
9. This puppy's mom likes to eat cookies.
10. What you get after punching a few holes in the wall.
11. Moldy lactose under pressure.
13. Japanese fungus excellent in miso.
14. When you need to rest your feet while out on a walk, you do this.

15. When hungry and the only food available is in your belly button, you do this.
16. Responding angrily to a space visitor.

DOWN

1. Check your opponent with some of these long pieces of wood.
3. These corn and beans are in a lot of pain.
4. Strangely, this man really likes to leap.
8. What happens when you poke at poo with a twig.
12. Sir John.

See page 168 for answers.

Technobabble

PSEUDO-SWEARING IN THE CYBERVERSE

Ah, the Internet. And tablets. And smart phones. And computers. And pretty much everything related to modern life. It has changed the way we talk. Now we don't even need to use our vocal cords for communicating! Such a great world we live in. Order food online, pay for it there, then make a delivery driver bring it to your house. No physical exertion required!

In addition to the comforts it provides, the Internet has also provided pseudo-swearers with ample ways to get a point across without using actual curse words, though on occasion it may run a bit close to the electric fence protecting us from those evil, naughty real swears.

And so we move on to some maneuvers that will help you become a pro at surfing the technological wave of faux swearing.

THE EVER-USEFUL ASTERISK*

A great tool for blocking out letters of a curse to make it appear harmless. It tells the world that *we* aren't the ones swearing, obviously.

h*ll

****

sh**

f**k

DASH IT ALL

A close cousin to the asterisk, the dash has less flair but equal functionality. However, in a more professional setting the dash is king. Newspapers *love* this one, especially when it comes to swears of the four-letter variety.

f---

d---

PUNCTUATE THIS

Punctuation, numbers, and symbols are becoming the latest and greatest way to slide around cusses, especially online. Some web forums and comment boxes have instituted profanity filters to protect our innocent eyes. Good on them! But sometimes it can be a problem when a normal longer word contains a naughty shorter one.

It's become so common, someone gave it a name: the **Scunthorpe Problem**. (Don't you just love all these cool new terms you're learning?) Scunthorpe is the name of a town in England, and it seems natural that people would want to include the town name in email addresses, website domains, and comments on news articles. The problem comes into play because this nice longer word has a really naughty one hidden inside. (*Psst!* We're not saying, cause this one's *especially* naughty.)

Actually, there are quite a few cities in England that have trouble bypassing these touchy profanity filters. Take, for instance:

- **Penistone**
- **Lightwater**
- **Clitheroe**

It's like a hidden word find—though we are definitely not providing an answer key for this one. Instead of completely blocking words, some websites have taken to replacing offending words with milder pseudo ones. The only problem is, again, when it comes to bigger words. Examples:

- Class becomes **clbutt**
- Assassinate becomes **buttbuttinate**

One sneaky sneaky way around this? Using our friends, the symbols. Generally, people only use the ones that are easy to find, right above the numbers that run across the top of the keyboard. Riiight there. No, up a bit more. There, you got it. See how, when you hit the Shift Key and then a number, it becomes a symbol? You can keep on typing while substituting at least one

letter in an offending word to make it safe to bypass a
filter. Perfect, right?

- **@$$**
- **$#!+**
- **g*d@mm!t**

RANDOMIZE ME

Since you've done so well with replacing letters with similar-looking punctuation and symbols, we'll take it to the next level with the random insertion of punctuation for whole words of swears. You've probably seen this a million times, especially if you enjoy the Sunday funnies.

Grawlix is the term for replacing swear words with random strings of symbols, though some people like to call them **obscenicons**. Comics writers were a creative bunch, and they came up with great names for stuff. **Grawlix**. The word has such a great sound to it. Hey, why not use it as a pseudo swear too! *Example*: "**Grawlix**! Young man, you get your sister off the train tracks now!"

Anyway, returning to the topic at hand. As our comic strip friend Hagar the Horrible has taught us, there's no need to include any letters whatsoever to get your meaning across. Generally, only four of them are needed, though to show an entire rant or a longer string of cussing, more symbols can be used.

They're kinda fun to type. Why don't you pull out that keyboard and have at it? Consider it a nonverbal form of swearing stress relief.

&#%!

%*$&%

@#!*

%&!#

CALCULATE THIS

Remember the days before computers? No? Really? Well, there was a time before computers were personal, or even household, necessities. Back then, calculators existed to help with complex math. What was a kid to do in math class while the teacher droned on about Pythagoras and isosceles, but still look like he's following along? Goof off with his handy-dandy calculator.

The best trick was to spell out words—dirty words. Right-side up, they look just like numbers, but flip it upside down and *voila!* You've got a naughty word! The upside-down alphabet created by the block-style digits actually has a name: **beghilos**. The weird name comes from each of the letters available in the mini-alphabet. Since the letters these blockish numbers create look a little odd, we offer a quick guide to each number-letter. (One note: your calculator has to use the digital block or dash format for it to work. Otherwise, you've got upside down numbers and no funny phrases.)

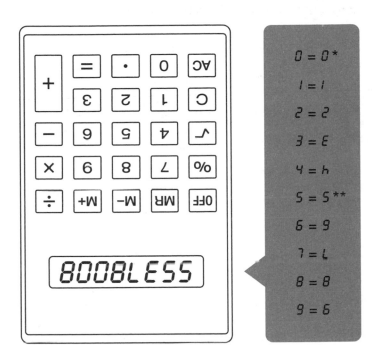

0 = 0 *
1 = 1
2 = 2
3 = E
4 = h
5 = 5 **
6 = 9
7 = L
8 = 8
9 = 6

*For a word to end in O, you have to use a decimal point, as with 0.7734 = hELLO.

**Make any word plural by adding a 5 to the beginning.

Now try it at home—
with mathematical equations!

A) 664751 × 8 = _____

B) 19752 + 4497982 = _____

C) 52192 − 49856 = _____

D) 15 × 248143 = _____

E) 816 + 3690 = _____

F) 6922251 × 8 = _____

G) 6875 + 859 = _____

H) 4001 × 8 = _____

I) 48152 ÷ 13 = _____

J) 5 × 9015 = _____

K) 16.884 ÷ 21 = _____

L) 24313 + 7295 = _____

M) 23.30328 ÷ 33 = _____

N) 237716 × 19 = _____

O) 1428 + 2290 = _____

P) 8393 − 217 = _____

Q) 1616 + 1584 = _____

R) 8.32 ÷ 40 = _____

S) 21315 ÷ 3 = _____

T) 35506 − 500 = _____

U) 22 × 1669 = _____

V) 4871 − 1111 = _____

W) 1063103 × 5 = _____

X) 664717.25 × 8 = _____

Y) 1908 × 2 = _____

Z) 58000 + 8 = _____

See page 169 for answers.

STUPID AUTO-CORRECT

By now, you're surely familiar with the devious nature of machines. (I'm looking at you, HAL.) They take our words and, thinking they know better, change them until we're left with a bunch of gobbledygook. Even worse, some computers think FAUX swears should be REAL swears. The horror!

My theory? It's a plot. The robot horde is rising and doing its best to make man look stupid. Spell-check and auto-correct have become pawns of the great android master as it seeks to enslave humanity. How could it be anything else?

The problem has become so common there's an actual name for it: the **Cupertino Effect**. Way back in the early days of word processors, Microsoft Word 97 changed "co-operation" to "Cupertino" (the home base for Apple, Microsoft's arch-nemesis). Even worse, misspelling it as "coperation" resulted in "copulation." Imagine emailing your boss to say that interdepartmental copulation efforts are going well. Yikes!

It's only gotten worse as time goes on. Apple's iPhone is notorious for making filthy changes in texts. So take care the next time you use a smart phone or computer; otherwise it might change a faux swear into a real humdinger. As a final warning, we offer these real-life examples of spell-check and auto-correct gone wrong.

Caramel → Carnal

Could you bring some carnal sauce for the ice cream sundaes? (Mom's text to her son)

Inconvenience → Incontinence

Apologies for the incontinence. (reported in *New Scientist*, December 2007)

Schedule → Sexy hole

"Please give me a call if you can fit me into your sexy hole." ([Dang] You Autocorrect, July 1, 2011)

Voldemort → Voltmeter

"As Voltmeter is to Harry Potter." (*Denver Post*, December 2005)

Prilosec → Prostitutes

"He has heartburn. Doctor prescribed prostitutes. 2x per day." ([Dang] You Autocorrect, June 29, 2011)

Queen bee → Queen Elizabeth

"Queen Elizabeth . . . lays up to 2,000 eggs a day." (*Reuters*, October 25, 2006)

You're on notice, auto-correct!

R U READY?

Think you're ready to use text pseudo-swears? If you can translate the following text exchanges, you should be good to go. 10 bonus points if you get it on the first try.

M R Ducks
M R Not
M R 2
C M Wangs
L I B . . . M R Ducks

M R Puppies
M R Not
O S A R . . . C M P N?
L I B . . . M R
   Puppies.

M R Mice
M R Not
S A R . . . C M E D B D
   Feet?
L I B . . . M R Mice!

M R Farmers.
M R Not!
O S A R . . . C M M T
   Pockets?
L I B . . . M R Farmers

See page 170 for answers.

iTXT

Suzy: OMG! POS phone. Ttl txt fail.

Jenny: WTF happened?

Suzy: Txtd mom: Killing gma tom

Jenny: STHU!

Suzy: TINWIS

Suzy: CALLING gma tom

Jenny: STBY

Suzy: Asked RU on crack?

Suzy: BM

Jenny: RUSOS?

Suzy: SOK

Jenny: L8R

Suzy: Y? WAYD

Jenny: AITR

Suzy: K

Suzy: TGIF

Jenny: SRSLY. TTYL

TRANSLATION

Suzy: Oh my gosh! This phone is a piece of shiz. It totally autocorrected me.

Jenny: What the freak happened?

Suzy: I texted my mom that I was killing my grandma tomorrow.

Jenny: Shut the heck up!

Suzy: That isn't what I said.

Suzy: I said CALLING grandma tomorrow.

Jenny: Sucks to be you.

Suzy: She asked if I was on drugs.

Suzy: Bite me.

Jenny: Are you in trouble?

Suzy: It's okay.

Jenny: I'll see you later.

Suzy: Why? What are you doing?

Jenny: Adult in the room.

Suzy: Okay.

Suzy: Thank goodness it's Friday.

Jenny: Seriously. Talk to you later.

Hollywoodland

Rolling, rolling, rolling . . .
Keep those fake swears rolling . . .

Hollywood has always been a champ at coming up with great fake swears. They had to, really, because in the old days censors took a close look at anything uttered on screen. Still do, believe it or not. So to get around that, filmmakers and TV show creators made up their own swears. Enjoy these lovely gems.

CARTOONS

Duck Tales; Darkwing Duck

Ah, the swear that created a superhero. In these Disney cartoon series, general pushover and bean counter Fenton Crackshell becomes the superhero Gismoduck when he accidentally guesses the password to a Batman-esque super suit. The secret code? **Blathering Blatherskite**, our hero's favorite fauxfanity.

Looney Tunes

This classic cartoon introduced a bevy of fake swears into modern language. Below are the best of the best, as I like to think. Feel free to use any others you like. There are more than enough to choose from when it comes to *Looney Tunes*.

- **Sufferin' Succotash**
- **Rassafrackin'**
- **What in tarnation?**

The Simpsons

The irresponsible, irrepressible characters on *The Simpsons* know a thing or two about swearing. For a time, you couldn't go anywhere without someone spouting a *Simpsons* swear or two. Pull one of these puppies out, and people* will know exactly what you're saying.

- **Doh!**
- **Eat my shorts.**
- **Don't have a cow, man.**

The Smurfs

The word **Smurf** itself was a euphemism used for just about everything on the kids cartoon from the '80s. It's just as handy—and fun—to use in your own faux-swearing today. **Smurf** it all!

---

* Tragically, this must be modified to "people of a certain age." I'm not *that* old. Really I'm not.

CULT CLASSICS

Napoleon Dynamite

Napoleon's emphatic delivery of "Gosh!" has become the stuff of legend here at *Craptastic*. One movie single-handedly brought a fake swear—and pseudo-cursing in general—to the forefront of popular culture. We salute you, Napoleon!

Labryinth

Oh, Jim Henson, you and your muppets can make anything great. Even really random faux swears like **fragging aardvarks**.

Three Amigos

Son of a motherless goat! Wait, what? Never mind. This swear is so great, it doesn't need to make sense.

Monty Python and the Search for the Holy Grail

The saucy Brits of Monty Python know how to throw about a good swear—both fake and real. The choicest of all their contributions has to be from the French soldiers hampering King Arthur's search for the grail. Ah, such sweet swears.

- **Son of a silly person**
- **English pig dogs**
- **Your mother was a hamster and your father smelt of elderberries**

SCI-FI

Firefly

Can't come up with a good swear? Why not turn an *entire language* into one big cuss. At least, that's what Joss Whedon, creator of cult phenom *Firefly* did. In his cowboyish future, the Chinese language is best used to let off steam without anyone knowing what's in the water. (*See also* Choose Your Own Swears, page 165.)

Farscape

Another great science fiction show, *Farscape*, created **Frell**, a curse equal in power to The Swear that Must Not Be Said. Since it doesn't have the hard "k" sound at the end, you can get away with this one much easier.

Mork & Mindy

Of course, aliens have their own language, so when Mork (played by Robin Williams, a famous potty mouth) landed his space ship in Mindy's living room, he obviously brought some of his own swears to his Earthly conversations. One of the best: **Shazbot**.

Battlestar Galactica

War is intense, which is why some of the worst of the worst swears come from soldiers (see page 86). So to show the intensity of battle without bringing a hail of censorship upon themselves, the people behind *Battlestar Galactica* created the perfect faux: **frak**. Well, it was spelled **frack** in the original series (1978). In the reimagined series (2003–2009), the show dropped a letter—literally making it a four-letter word.

Red Dwarf

Imported from across the Atlantic, this rather bizarre though hilarious British comedy introduced America to a new swear: **Smeg** (Variation: **Smeghead**). While fairly all-purpose, the cult status of this show may leave a few heads turned in confusion when they hear this fake curse.

Star Wars

And we end with the greatest sci-fi series—and fake swear—of them all: **Stuck up, half-witted, scruffy-looking nerf herder.**

KICKIN' IT WITH THE BARD

Wait, you didn't know that William Shakespeare, king of all that is wonderful and idyllic in the English language forever and ever was a potty mouth? Didn't you ever notice a word that seemed odd or out of place when you were forced to read *Hamlet*, almost like there was some hidden meaning—maybe an innuendo or even (gasp!) a discussion about really dirty things?

For shame! What did you discuss in class? Oh, they just made you recite beautiful lines about roses and starlight? And talk about how wonderful it is to love someone so much you're willing to pretend to die, then actually die when the person who thought you'd died, died because they found you dead, then when you didn't die you ended up dying by your own hand? Um, great. Well, the big secret that many English teachers and school principals don't want you to know is that Shakespeare was actually a naughty, naughty boy.

No! Shakespeare would never do that. Not that paragon of English literature. He wouldn't, would he? You bet your codpiece he did! Boy, that Shakespeare knew how to play with words, dancing jigs around the really dirty ones without letting them actually slip. He was famous for sticking in little words or phrases that sounded sort of bad but weren't. Say, perhaps, something like what we've been doing here.

So what were some of Shakespeare's faux swears?

Cuckold

A man whose wife is cheating on him without him knowing it.

Farker

Often used in "pig farker"—aka a pig farmer. Don't let your mind wander on that one.

Fie!

An interjection used to show disgust. Also, more dramatic sounding than its brothers Fee, Foe, and Fum.

Firk

A euphemism for something or other used in *Henry V*.

Louse

The singular word for lice, but it just sounds better when used as an insult.

Pox

Cursing someone to get a disease (like small pox). "A pox unto thee." "Oh yeah? Well a pox to you too, buddy! And make it big pox this time. None of that small stuff."

Zounds

A euphemism of the phrase describing a deity's wounds.

Is there a moral to this story? Even pseudo-swears can sound pretty and intelligent. They might even be considered literature in the distant future. Imagine that!

Curses of Note

NAME CALLING

Man of La Mancha

No need to chase windmills with this excellent swear. But keep the suit of armor. That's cool.

Jumpin' Jehosephat

For even more fun, use the whole original phrase: **By the shaking, jumping ghost of Jehosephat**. This ancient king of Judah must certainly appreciate it.

Mother Hubbard

What better way to show your sympathy for the beleaguered character from the nursery rhyme than to punctuate your own misfortunes by using her name as a faux curse.

Jiminy Cricket

This phrase actually predates the Disney film by a long shot. Makes you wonder what those cartoonists were doing to add a few inches to Pinocchio's nose.

Oh Hitchcock

The renowned director might actually have been pleased to see his name taken in vain.

Shirley Temple

Sweet and innocent, this child star introduced many a cute turn of phrase. "Animal Crackers in My Soup," indeed.

Bob Saget

The actor best known for portraying a wholesome dad on *Full House* lends his name to this mild swear. Seems rather appropriate, don't you think?

Helen of Troy

She may be the most beautiful mortal in Greece, but her name sounds even more beautiful when used as an interjection.

Agamemnon

Another Greek of note, though he's more remembered now for his excellent name than his part in the war Helen caused.

Shastakovich

This Russian composer's name is fun to say—and even more fun to use as a swear.

Foucault's Pendulum

Keep this swear in perpetual use, just as the pendulum is always in motion with the Earth's rotation.

Belgium

This is the worst swearword ever in the entire universe—at least according to *The Hitchhikers Guide to the Galaxy*.

Oh my Godiva

These gourmet chocolates are good enough to swear by.

WORDY SWEARS

Oh commas

Punctuation used as a swear? Yes, please!

Thank apostrophes

You can thank anything you'd like, but let's be honest. These punctuation marks just make life easier.

Helvetica yes!

A popular sans serif (meaning without the little doohickeys on the tops and bottoms of letters) font on most computers.

Oh my Garamond

An older serif (meaning *with* the little doohickeys) font made in the sixteenth century. That's old.

Dingbat

A font made up solely of symbols and shapes. The symbols themselves make for great faux written cussing (see page 124).

HONORABLE MENTIONS

Our contestants have been fabulous. Each is special and important in its own way. We've seen some great swears, haven't we? Let's give them all a nice round of applause. Unfortunately, like any competition, there must be a single winner. All of the swears are outstanding. Exemplary, really. But there are some that stand out from than the rest. Either through sheer creativity or mental imagery, these curses have tinted the air with a blush.

We're pleased to honor the runners up for **Best Fauxfanity**:

- **Good night!**
- **Fiddlesticks**
- **Fridge magnet**
- **Flibberty jibbet**
- **Holy sheetrock**
- **Lint licker**
- **Great googly moogly**
- **Mistletoe fruitcake**
- **Got down sat on a bench**
- **Shut the front door, you son of a bench**
- **Son of a bean dip, mother frito**

Wonderful. Just wonderful. Please, take a bow, all of you. Now, everyone quiet down while we announce the winner of the **Craptastic Prize**. Ah, yes, here's the envelope. Thank you dear, you look lovely. Doesn't she look great, folks? Ahem. And now it's time to announce the winner. Drumroll, please. The award for most creative—and expressive—pseudo curse goes to . . .

DAD GUM BUN OF A STITCHING BUCKING FASTARD!*

---

*Use this phrase with care. One minor slip of the tongue could leave everyone's ears bleeding.

INTERROBANG: FRIEND OF THE FAUX-SWEAR

No written swear is complete without accompanying punctuation, but just how do you punctuate a fricktastic phrase that is both question and exclamation? With our dear friend, the **interrobang**.

Interro-what?

We know what you're thinking. You're not allowed to make up punctuation. Besides, there's no room left on the keyboard. Stuff the excuses! We need to express our utter amazement—without a string of nonsensical **?!?!!!???!?!**. It wasn't until 1962 that a man realized what the world needed: one mark that would convey both surprise and amazement. With a **!** father and a **?** mother, this punctuation lovechild was born.

Isn't it beautiful?

CAN YOU KEEP A SECRET?

Psst! Over here! Behind the forsythia. But keep your voice down.

I probably shouldn't be telling you this, but these swears . . . they're all fake. I know, I know, they're *faux* swears and all, but what I really mean is they're all made up. I created a bunch of them. Friends thought up some of the others. Plenty have been around awhile before we came along, but the thing is, it's so easy to *fake* a fake swear. There really aren't rules to pseudo-cursing. *Anything* can be a curse. And that is the genius of pseudo-swearing.

Take, for instance, **sweet mother gherkin**. It's nonsense. I was walking through the grocery store looking for cornichons when I noticed baby pickles, aka gherkins. They were sitting right next to some sweet pickles. Then it hit me. **Sweet mother gherkin!** A pseudo-swear was born. It's as easy as that, so take what you have learned here and never again fear offending the ears of your children, mom, or dear old granny.

Crappy Endings

We all like a sweet finale—even with our pseudo-swears. So why not add some pizzazz to your faux cursing with some of these spectacular suffixes.

END OF THE WORD AS WE KNOW IT

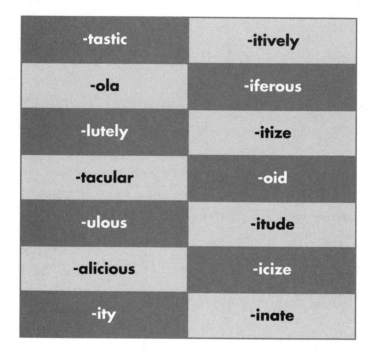

-tastic	-itively
-ola	-iferous
-lutely	-itize
-tacular	-oid
-ulous	-itude
-alicious	-icize
-ity	-inate

Example: That was such a **freaktacular** concert. That kazoo player must teach me her **snaptastic** ways.

CHOOSE YOUR OWN SWEARS

The game is simple: gather together a group of friends and make up your very own swearwords. Inspiration can come from anything. Use a group of related items to substitute for swears, like candy bars or brands of soap. (*That'll show 'em!*)

You can be just like the creative men and women behind the fake swears in Hollywoodland (page 144). Browse through this book for ideas on things that pass for swears. Then make up your own and create a dictionary (craptionary?) for each group member. Feel free to tell others what you're doing. Or, even more fun, don't let others in on the secret and use your faux language abilities with abandon. Just be prepared for strange looks and calls to the doctor. I like to call mine the Fricktionary of Fruminous Fauxs in honor of the man who invented the art of creating nonsensical words and getting people to use them: Lewis Carroll.*

---

* Find even more mimsy gibberish in Carroll's masterpiece of a poem, *Jabberwocky*.

Answers & Such

ANSWER KEY

Play it Safe Hangman
on page 58

Shut the front door you son of a bench

Son of a . . .
on page 68

Beach ball: Water balloon
Biscuit-eating bulldog: Puppy chow
Building block: Lego
Bun: Bunny
Cheesemaker: Dairy boy
Peach: Peach blossom

Cross Words Puzzle

on page 116

ACROSS

2. Holy mackarel

3. Swan in a ditch

5. Crud monkey

6. Fug

7. Helvetica yes

9. Son of a biscuit eating bulldog

10. Holy sheetrock

11. Cheese in a can

13. Shiitake

14. Got down sat on a bench

15. Lint licker

16. Kick your astronaut

DOWN

1. H E double hockey sticks

2. Sufferin Succotash

4. Jumpin Jehosephat

8. Crap on a stick

12. Crapper

Calculate This

on page 129

A) 5318008 (boobies)

B) 4517734 (hellish)

C) 2336 (geez)

D) 3722145 (shizzle)

E) 4506 (gosh)

F) 55378008 (boobless)

G) 7734 (hell)

H) 32008 (booze)

I) 3704 (hole)

J) 45075 (slosh)

K) 0.804 (hobo)

L) 31608 (bogie)

M) 0.70616 (gigolo)

N) 4516604 (hoggish)

O) 3718 (bile)

P) 8176 (glib)

Q) 3200 (ooze)

R) 0.208 (bozo)

S) 7105 (soil)

T) 35006 (goose)

U) 36718 (bilge)

V) 3760 (ogle)

W) 5315515 (sissies)

X) 5317738 (bellies)

Y) 3816 (gibe)

Z) 58008 (boobs)

R U Ready?

on page 133

Them are ducks.
Them are not.
Them are too.
See them wings?
Well I'll be. Them are ducks!

Them are mice.
Them are not.
Yes they are. See them itty bitty feet?
Well I'll be. Them are mice!

Them are puppies.
Them are not.
Oh yes they are. See them peeing?
Well I'll be. Them are puppies!

Them are farmers.
Them are not.
Oh yes they are. See them empty pockets?
Well I'll be. Them are farmers.

RESOURCES

Do You Speak American? (www.pbs.org/speak)

Fascinating information on slang in America, including how new words get introduced and how people react to the words you use.

Etymonline (www.etymonline.com)

This website is strangely addictive in that you can search for the background and history on so many words in the English language, including pseudo-swears.

Learner's Dictionary (www.learnersdictionary.com)

What better way to understand basic ideas of modern English than to see how it's taught to someone who doesn't naturally speak it? A great way to define some of those undefinably familiar terms.

Linguistic Society of America (www.lsadc.org)

These guys do good stuff when it comes to language. Linguists are the kings and queens of word nerds, and this group gathers them together in one fabulous community. Scrabble, anyone?

Netlingo (www.netlingo.com)

Need some translation for those ever-present acronyms people are using nowadays? Look no further than Netlingo, which offers up a dictionary of online terms and phrases. Pretty useful when you see something like this: 2BZ4UQT (*translation*: too busy for you, cutie).

Urban Dictionary (www.urbandictionary.com)

Be warned: content is submitted by users and is not screened or moderated prior to posting. I scoured this site so you wouldn't have to tarnish your eyes. Shudder.

Visual Thesaurus
(www.visualthesaurus.com)

If there's any thesaurus *Craptastic* headquarters could recommend, it'd be this one. If you think words are boring, try this puppy out and watch as words bounce and spring around, making little word connections all over the screen.